LOVE NOTES TO SELF

A GUIDED JOURNAL FOR SELF-LOVE AND HEALING

Printed in the United States of America.

ISBN: 979-8-9870149-3-6 (Paperback)

To every beautiful soul that holds this book:

You are enough, just as you are at this very moment. May these pages remind you of this truth every day.

HELLO.

INTRODUCTION

Hey there! For as long as I can remember, I've believed in the transformative power of journaling and its role in cultivating self-love. That's why I created *Love Notes To Self.*

This journal is a heartfelt tool to guide you in embracing and celebrating your worth and offering a space for reflection and growth.

Picture this: each day, you get to sit back, pen in hand, and rediscover the extraordinary person you are. Loving yourself is the foundation of your well-being and happiness; it affects how you view yourself, navigate relationships, and cope with life's challenges.

By practicing self-love, you cultivate a positive self-image, build resilience, and create a nurturing inner dialogue. Trust me, it is so important to acknowledge our worth, especially as we navigate the complexities of our paths and the ups and downs of being human.

I believe you were drawn to this book because somewhere within, you recognize the importance of nurturing and valuing yourself. Perhaps you're at a point in life where you're seeking deeper self-understanding or learning to be more compassionate toward yourself.

This book can be an invaluable support in this journey. My wish is that as you journal, you'll discover and embrace the full extent of your amazing qualities and inherent worthiness.

A few years ago, I found myself at what felt like the lowest point in my life. I was hospitalized twice during the COVID-19 pandemic for gallbladder and appendix removal, trapped in a toxic relationship, and engulfed by a deep sense of depression. However, when I chose to prioritize my happiness and embrace self-love, my world transformed dramatically. There is indeed life and love after pain – I am living proof of that. Today, I am happy, healthy, and deeply committed to self-love every single day. I've found my purpose in creating journals like this, aiming to empower women worldwide with the message: "You've got this, and we've got each other."

My healing and self-love journey began with simple, inspirational notes to myself and sticking them around my apartment. These small acts of self-love turned my entire day around.

In this journal, I pass this practice on to you, offering a daily note to self, designed to transform self-love into a daily habit. I recommend repeating these affirmations and mantras because they are a powerful tool that will gradually reshape your thoughts, strengthen your self-belief, and manifest a life filled with love and positivity.

Love Notes To Self is filled with daily affirmations, insightful journaling prompts, and empowering exercises to nurture self-compassion. I want to remind you that the most epic love story is where you fall head over heels for yourself.

This journey is yours to navigate – you can explore these pages in chronological order (one day at a time), or you can let your intuition guide you, opening to a random page and trusting that the message you find is exactly what you need at that moment.

As you dive into the pages, let's make a pact to be kinder to ourselves, okay?

It's time we recognized our awesomeness and took solid steps in our personal development because **self-love isn't selfish — it is essential.**

Amber James
xoxo

Author, Creator of Notes To Self Shop

Day 1

I am enough just as I am.

DEFINING SELF LOVE

Self-love is valuing yourself, caring for your well-being, and accepting who you are at your core. It's about recognizing your worth independent of external achievements, respecting yourself, and acknowledging your needs and feelings.

The daily practice of self-love means setting boundaries, forgiving yourself, celebrating your strengths, and embracing your weaknesses with compassion. It's a lifelong commitment to being your own best friend and cheerleader.

In a world that often tells you to be more, do more, or change more, here's a gentle reminder: You are a complete and beautiful person with unique strengths, vulnerabilities, and experiences. Embrace your journey with kindness and remember **you are enough** just by being you.

A wonderful mentor once shared with me that just like an athlete trains, self-love requires regular attention and care. Each day presents a new opportunity to nurture it, whether through affirmations or self-care routines. It's about showing kindness and patience, even on days when it feels challenging.

List ten things that you absolutely love about yourself.

♥
. . . .
♥
. . . .
♥
. . . .
♥
. . . .
♥
. . . .
♥
. . . .
♥
. . . .
♥
. . . .
♥
. . . .
♥
. . . .

> **Write today's affirmation five times.**
>
> **"I am enough just as I am."**

NOTES TO SELF

_____

_____

_____

_____

_____

_____

_____

_____

_____

_____

_____

_____

_____

_____

_____

_____

Day 2

I am deserving
of happiness.

OWN YOUR HAPPINESS

It's common for many of us to fall into the mindset that happiness is something to be earned. We often tell ourselves, "I'll be happy when I get that promotion," or "I'll feel fulfilled once I'm in a relationship." This pursuit leads us on an endless chase, where happiness is always just out of reach.

I remember a time when I was solely focused on climbing the corporate ladder, believing that my value was directly linked to my job title and salary. Despite my achievements, a sense of fulfillment eluded me. Only when I reflected on my inner self did I discover the missing piece. I started to appreciate my qualities beyond my professional success - my kindness, creativity, and resilience. I realized my worth was not something I had to prove or earn.

Embracing this mindset was liberating. I began to find joy in simple everyday moments and in being myself, rather than in external validations. This didn't mean abandoning my goals or aspirations but rather pursuing them with a different mindset - one where my happiness and self-worth were not on the line with every step I took.

I'm standing here as a friend now, reminding you that **you are worthy of happiness** and don't need to do anything special to deserve it, okay? It's yours, just by being you.

I am worthy of happiness because...

Write today's affirmation five times.

"I am deserving of happiness."

NOTES TO SELF

_____

_____

_____

_____

_____

_____

_____

_____

_____

_____

_____

_____

_____

_____

_____

_____

_____

_____

Day 3

I choose to speak to myself with love and compassion.

WORDS ARE POWERFUL

The way you talk to yourself shapes your reality. Words carry power, and the ones you choose to use toward yourself can either uplift or weigh you down. I remember a particularly challenging day at work when a project I was leading hit an unexpected snag. Frustrated, I muttered under my breath, "I'm such an idiot."

Hearing this, a co-worker, with concern in her eyes, said, "Stop that. Would you ever say that to a friend facing a tough situation? You are so smart and amazing."

This comment stopped me in my tracks. I realized my self-criticism was not only harsh but also something I would never direct towards someone else. This moment highlighted the double standard I had for myself versus how I treated others.

From then on, I tried to treat myself with the same compassion and understanding I would offer a friend or someone I loved. Now, when things don't go as planned, instead of resorting to self-deprecation, I offer words of encouragement to myself: "Everyone makes mistakes" or "You can learn and grow from this."

When you talk to yourself with compassion and understanding, you nurture your self-esteem and foster a positive mindset, so **choose words wisely.**

Imagine your inner critic is now your inner cheerleader. Write five things this cheerleader would say to you during a tough day.

NOTES TO SELF

_____

_____

_____

_____

_____

_____

_____

_____

_____

_____

_____

_____

_____

_____

_____

_____

_____

Day 4

I am gorgeous!

HELLO, GORGEOUS!

In case no one told you today, I wanted to remind you of how **absolutely amazing you are.** Seriously, you shine brightly, and sometimes, I don't think you realize how much you light up the world around you.

First off, your beauty – inside and out – is simply stunning. You have this natural glow that's about more than looks; your energy and kindness make you truly beautiful.

You have this way of making everyone around you feel better just by being you. It's a gift, and you should never underestimate its power.

But more than anything, your kind heart sets you apart. Never forget how much you're loved and appreciated.

Keep being your awesome self!

List four qualities you love about your appearance.

♥
· ·

♥
· ·

♥
· ·

♥
· ·

♥ ♥ ♥

List five traits you value about your character.

♥
· ·

♥
· ·

♥
· ·

♥
· ·

Write today's affirmation five times.

"I am gorgeous."

NOTES TO SELF

Day 5

I am patient with myself.

GROWTH TAKES TIME

When I first took up tennis, I wasn't the best player. My serves often went wild, and my backhand was more of a hit-or-miss. Initially, it was frustrating. I would watch others play so effortlessly while I struggled to keep the ball in play. There were moments when I thought of giving up, feeling embarrassed about my skill level compared to others.

Then, during one particularly challenging match, I was on the verge of throwing in the towel, but my coach pulled me aside and shared that the best players weren't born great; they grew great through persistence and self-belief. He saw something in me that I was blind to – not just potential in tennis, but the **resilience** and **determination** to improve and succeed.

Gradually, my skills began to improve. My serves became more controlled, and my backhand started to find its mark more often than not.

It's easy to be hard on ourselves. But what if we shifted our mindset and were more patient with ourselves? This approach is about creating a balance where we strive for our goals without harsh self-judgment and understanding that setbacks are not permanent.

Think of an area in your life where you tend to be hard on yourself. What can you do to show yourself more love?

> **Write today's affirmation five times.**
>
> **"I am patient with myself."**

NOTES TO SELF

_____

_____

_____

_____

_____

_____

_____

_____

_____

_____

_____

_____

_____

_____

_____

_____

_____

_____

Day 6

I accept my awesomeness.

YOU (YES, YOU) ARE SO AWESOME!

Let's try a little fun exercise. Stand up, take a deep breath, and confidently say, **"I accept my awesomeness."** How does that feel? Now, repeat it a few more times.

Initially, speaking affirmations out loud might feel awkward or even a bit silly. However, as you continue this practice regularly, it gradually becomes more natural.

And it's good for your health, too! Scientific studies have shown that repeating positive affirmations can rewire our brains to think more positively, boosting self-esteem and overall mental well-being. So, keep at it; the more you do it, the more you'll start to believe and embody these affirmations. When we accept our awesomeness, we give ourselves permission to be our most authentic selves. We stop shrinking ourselves to fit into boxes and start living life on our terms. This authenticity brings us joy and attracts people who love and appreciate us for who we truly are.

Now, let's repeat the affirmation again: "I accept my awesomeness."

What compliment(s) do you give to people? Give it to yourself. How does it make you feel?

NOTES TO SELF

_____

_____

_____

_____

_____

_____

_____

_____

_____

_____

_____

_____

_____

_____

_____

_____

Day 7

I trust my intuition.

TRUST YOUR GUT

Intuition is that inner wisdom, a subtle yet powerful guiding force that helps us navigate life's complexities. It's often described as a gut feeling, a hunch, or a sixth sense. Intuition is our subconscious mind processing information and experiences at a speed the conscious mind cannot match. But **why trust intuition?**

Our intuition is shaped by our past experiences, our deepest values, and our truest selves. It cuts through the noise of external influences and touches the core of our being, offering guidance that aligns with our true desires and needs. The first step to trusting your intuition is learning to listen to it, which requires us to slow down.

The logical mind loves facts and evidence, and when intuition leads us in a direction without these, doubt creeps in. Overcoming this doubt involves a leap of faith — a trust in the knowledge that our inner self understands more than we realize.

When we start making decisions based on our intuition, life feels more authentic and often leads to unexpected but fulfilling outcomes, opening doors we didn't even know existed.

Think about a time when you trusted
your gut, and it led to a positive outcome.
What were the feelings that guided you?
How did it feel to trust yourself?

Write today's affirmation five times.

"I trust my intuition."

NOTES TO SELF

_____

_____

_____

_____

_____

_____

_____

_____

_____

_____

_____

_____

_____

_____

_____

_____

_____

Day 8

I am courageous and brave.

BE BOLD. BE BRAVE.

Throughout life, we encounter moments that challenge us, push us out of our comfort zones, and require us to summon strength we didn't know we had. In these times, reminding ourselves of **our inherent courage and bravery** can be incredibly powerful.

For me, leaving a toxic relationship was one of the hardest decisions I ever had to make. The beginning was beautiful, as most stories of love are. But as time passed, I found myself constantly trying to please my partner and hoping to fix things that were beyond repair. I had poured so much time, energy, and emotion into this relationship that walking away felt daunting. *Would I ever find love again?* I wondered, knowing deep down that this wasn't the life I wanted for myself. It required every ounce of bravery I possessed.

Looking back, I am so glad I trusted myself and didn't settle. This moment taught me the importance of self-love and self-respect; it showed me that sometimes, the most courageous act is not to hold on, but to let go.

By releasing my ex, I've welcomed a world of new possibilities, paving the way for the healthy, loving partnership I have today.

Reflect on your personal qualities, strengths, and achievements. Write a list of affirmations starting with 'I am...' that celebrate these aspects of yourself.

"I AM..." SELF LOVE
WORD SEARCH

INSTRUCTIONS: SEARCH UP, DOWN, FORWARD, BACKWARD, AND DIAGONAL TO FIND THE HIDDEN WORDS.

```
G L O R I G I N A L I
E T Y E N B P A U E Y
N L R L O V E D G N E
E L W O R T H Y I O W
R Z R R N Y U I L U D
O E S U R G C S P G R
U F F D M T K L A H Y
S U L U C K Y R C N B
N O K I N D V K I N O
B R A V E J F U L K L
C R E A T I V E O Q D
```

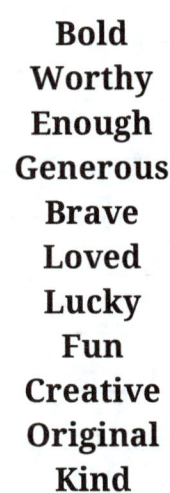

Bold
Worthy
Enough
Generous
Brave
Loved
Lucky
Fun
Creative
Original
Kind

NOTES TO SELF

Day 9

I treat my body with love and care.

CARING FOR YOUR BODY
=
CARING FOR YOUR SOUL

Treating your body with love and care goes beyond physical health and appearance. It's about developing a relationship of respect, kindness, and compassion with your body. This means listening to its needs, appreciating its uniqueness, and nurturing it, not just for aesthetic reasons, but for your overall well-being. **Your body is capable of amazing things, so take time to appreciate all it does for you.**

Celebrate its strengths and what it can achieve, whether that's through physical activity, relaxation, or simply being present in the moment. When you care for your body, you care for your soul. Unfortunately, social media, advertisements, and even well-meaning comments from others can sometimes magnify every pimple and curve, creating unrealistic standards.

So **be kind to yourself** and recognize that these natural, beautiful parts make you, you! Surround yourself with positive influences, and remember that self-love is a personal process that takes time and patience.

Think about the parts of your body you usually criticize. Write a short note of thanks to these parts, recognizing their value and expressing gratitude for them.

NOTES TO SELF

_____

_____

_____

_____

_____

_____

_____

_____

_____

_____

_____

_____

_____

_____

_____

_____

Day 10

I choose joy.

THE REMARKABLE
BENEFITS OF JOY

Did you know? Science backs the power of a joyful outlook!

Studies show that embracing joy and positivity can boost our mental and physical health. When we choose joy, we're not just feeling good in that moment; we're also nurturing our well-being in the long term. Positive emotions are linked to lower stress levels, better immune function, and even a longer life. It's like giving a wellness gift to ourselves every day!

By actively choosing to bring more joy into your life, you not only enhance your daily experiences but also create a positive cycle where more joyful moments show up. So, let's make a conscious choice to **find joy in our daily lives**. Whether it's savoring a morning coffee, enjoying a laugh with friends, or simply basking in a moment of peace, these joyful experiences add up to a healthier, happier you.

Create a list of things that bring you joy,
no matter how big or small. Then, reflect
on how you can incorporate more of
these experiences into your daily life.

Write today's affirmation five times.

"I choose joy."

NOTES TO SELF

Day 11

I release what no longer serves me.

LET IT GO

We're continually evolving, so it's important to periodically reassess what serves us. We often hold onto things far longer than we should – be it bad habits, relationships, thoughts, regrets, or emotions. Remember when I went through that tough breakup? It was a challenging period, but it taught me an invaluable lesson about the power of releasing things that don't serve our well-being.

It's not just about romantic relationships; this principle applies to various aspects of our lives - be it negative thoughts, toxic family members or friends, or even a job that fails to recognize our true value.

Take my bestie, Sara. She was in a job that made her feel undervalued and stressed. But the fear of change kept her stuck. Only when she finally decided to step out of her comfort zone and apply for other jobs did she find a company that celebrated her skills and allowed her to grow.

Letting go is essential for all of us because it makes space for better things. Sometimes it's uncomfortable, but the growth and peace that come from the process are worth it.

Identify what's holding you back from letting go. What fears or beliefs are in your way?

Today, I choose to let go of the things in my life that no longer serve me, including:

Write today's affirmation five times.

"I release what no longer serves me."

NOTES TO SELF

Day 12

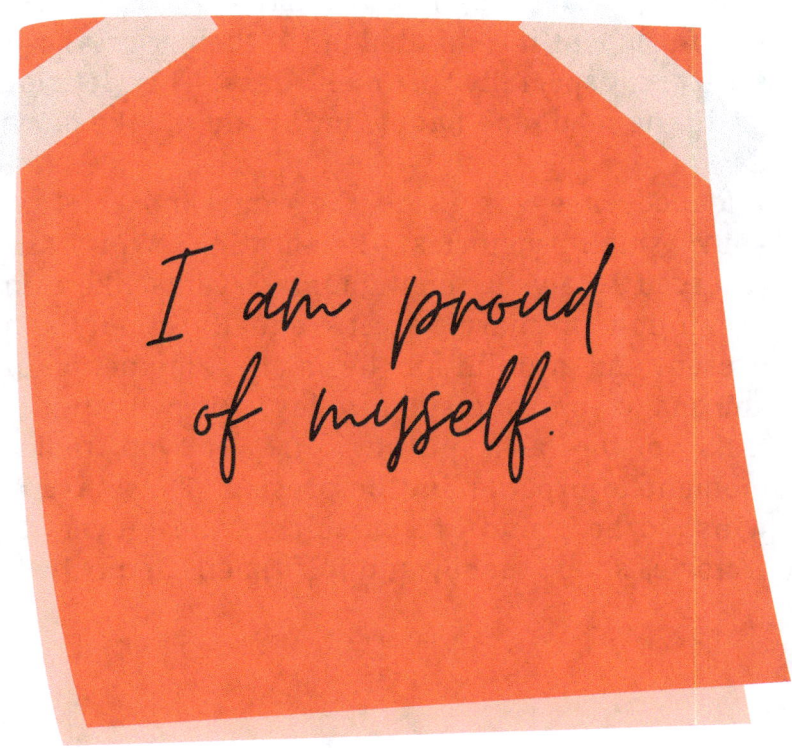

I am proud of myself.

CELEBRATE YOUR WINS

In a world that often focuses on what we haven't achieved, it's vital to pause and appreciate our wins, no matter how small they seem.

As I sat in my favorite coffee shop the other day, a sense of calm washed over me. I watched the sunrise, coffee in hand, and it struck me how significant these moments are. I'd been in a funk and wanted to stay in bed. But there I was, taking time for myself, something I often overlook. Getting out of bed and treating myself to a morning coffee might seem trivial, but it was a win for me, as it reminded me of the importance of self-care, especially on "meh" days. This delicious iced latte made me happy and ready to take on the day.

I encourage you to do the same and celebrate your small victories. Celebrating wins isn't reserved solely for monumental events like a big promotion or marriage; it's equally about being present and grateful for the smallest moments. Did you make someone smile today? Did you finish a task you've been putting off? Or you took a moment to breathe and be present. **These are all wins**, so be proud of yourself, as these everyday victories shape the joy and fulfillment in our lives.

List six accomplishments that you're proud of.

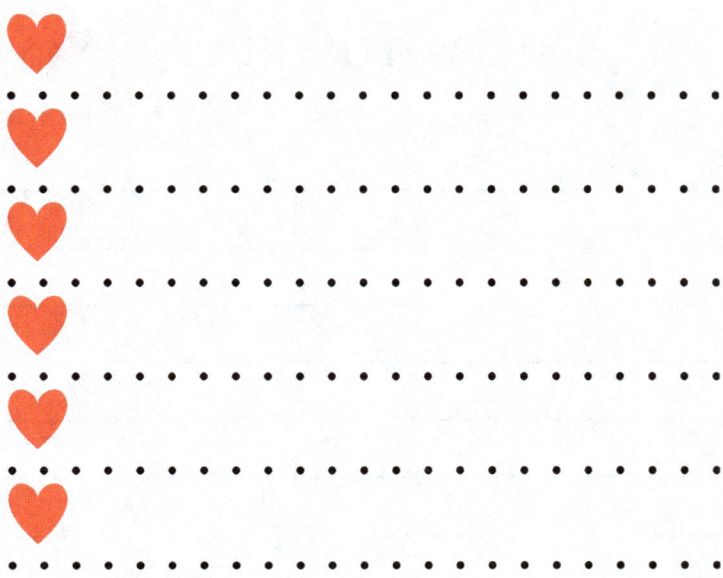

How did these milestones shape your personal or professional growth, and what did they teach you about yourself?

Write today's affirmation five times.

"I am proud of myself."

NOTES TO SELF

Day 13

My life is abundant.

ABUNDANCE MINDSET

Have you ever considered the impact of the words you use to describe your life? The idea behind affirmations like "My life is abundant" is rooted in the Law of Attraction, which suggests that our thoughts can shape our reality.

When we focus on abundance, we attract more of it into our lives. Conversely, if we dwell on what we lack, we may be stuck in a scarcity mindset.

It's essential to recognize that abundance extends beyond material wealth. It includes relationships, experiences, health, love, and inner peace. We foster a sense of gratitude and contentment by acknowledging and appreciating these aspects of our lives. It can also lead to a more positive outlook, where relationships can become more fulfilling, opportunities are everywhere, and challenges seem more manageable.

How can you incorporate this affirmation into your life? Start with daily repetition (make it the first thing you say when you wake up in the morning), do mindful reflection throughout your day, and incorporate journaling where you jot down things you're grateful for every day.

Imagine your ideal abundant life. What does it include, and what steps can you take today to move closer to this vision?

NOTES TO SELF

_____

_____

_____

_____

_____

_____

_____

_____

_____

_____

_____

_____

_____

_____

_____

_____

_____

Day 14

I am deserving of my own love and compassion.

BOOST SELF-COMPASSION

It's a common scenario: you're always there for others, offering a shoulder to lean on.

But when it comes to treating yourself with the same level of kindness, you might fall short. Here's a gentle reminder: **You are just as deserving of the love and compassion you so freely give to others.** Often, we are our own harshest critics, but imagine if you treated yourself the way you treated your best friend, with patience, kindness, and understanding. When you start to love yourself, something beautiful happens: you begin to see yourself in a more positive light; your self-esteem gets a boost, and you may find it easier to navigate life's ups and downs.

Here are a few ways to practice self-love:

- **Positive Self-Talk:** Next time you catch yourself being self-critical, reframe those thoughts in a kinder, more compassionate way.

- **Self-Care Rituals:** Whether it's a relaxing bath, a leisurely walk, or just quiet time with a book, make time for activities that nurture your soul.

How can you be your own hype woman every day?

NOTES TO SELF

_____

_____

_____

_____

_____

_____

_____

_____

_____

_____

_____

_____

_____

_____

_____

_____

_____

_____

Day 15

I am lovable just as I am.

KNOW YOUR WORTH

My dating experiences in NYC were quite a rollercoaster! There were so many times when I felt frustrated, especially when guys would ghost after just one or two dates. It was disheartening, and I often found myself questioning my worth.

But then, an incredible friend gave me a piece of advice that completely shifted my perspective. She said, "Instead of wondering if you're good enough for them, ask yourself if you like their company. **You're the prize**." What a game-changer!

This approach made dating much more enjoyable and less stressful. It's a reminder that I have value and don't need to settle for anyone who doesn't see that. If they choose to leave, it's their loss, not mine. I wanted to share this with you in case you ever find yourself in a similar boat. **You are lovable, just as you are**. Understanding this certainty frees us from the exhausting pursuit of trying to be something we're not and allows us to focus on being the best version of ourselves.

Not everyone will see or appreciate your value, and **that's okay**; their inability to see your worth doesn't diminish it.

Finish this sentence: "The kind of people
I want to surround myself with are..."

NOTES TO SELF

_____

_____

_____

_____

_____

_____

_____

_____

_____

_____

_____

_____

_____

_____

_____

_____

_____

Day 16

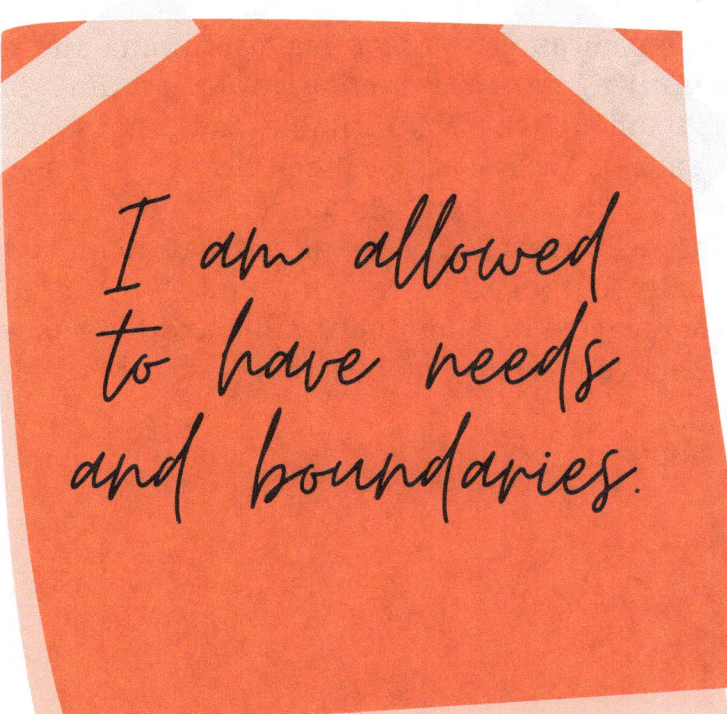

I am allowed
to have needs
and boundaries.

SET BETTER BOUNDARIES

For the longest time, I felt like having needs or setting boundaries was a sign of being demanding or difficult. But I realized it's actually **a sign of self-respect and self-care**, both in my professional and personal life.

At work, I finally learned to say no to excessive overtime, prioritizing my health and work-life balance. This improved my well-being and actually increased my productivity during working hours.

In my love life, I made it clear that consistent and respectful communication was non-negotiable. This meant no more accepting last-minute plans or tolerating the bare minimum. Expressing your needs about what's acceptable and what's not is essential. When we communicate our needs clearly, we create healthier, more honest relationships. Sure, it might feel uncomfortable initially, but it gets easier with time.

The people who genuinely value and love us will respect your needs - no questions asked.

What do you struggle with saying no to? What would happen if you did say no? Is this thought accurate or based on fear?

Write today's affirmation five times.

"I am allowed to have needs and boundaries."

NOTES TO SELF

_____
_____
_____
_____
_____
_____
_____
_____
_____
_____
_____
_____
_____
_____
_____
_____
_____

Day 17

I prioritize my peace.

FIND YOUR INNER PEACE

I wanted to share something that's been making a significant impact on my life lately. I've been consciously **focusing on what brings me tranquility and joy.** It's incredible how this simple shift in perspective has started to resonate through all aspects of my life. I have even noticed a ripple effect that flows into my work, relationships, and well-being.

For me, it is a quiet morning walk in nature or morning snuggles with my puppy. Slowing down or spending time alone, even if it's just 15 minutes, gives me the space to recharge. For you, it could be something entirely different. **The key is finding those things that resonate with you**.

Inner peace may also stem from small acts of setting boundaries, like asking a coworker to come back in ten minutes while you're finishing a project on a tight deadline. It's about honoring your current priorities and managing interruptions gracefully.

Similarly, not feeling compelled to text someone back immediately can be a form of self-care. It allows you to respond when you can give your full attention. Though seemingly minor, these moments play a role in maintaining a sense of calm in our lives.

What does prioritizing your peace mean to you? What actions can you take to ensure your well-being remains a priority?

PEACEFUL WORD SEARCH

INSTRUCTIONS: SEARCH UP, DOWN, FORWARD, BACKWARD, AND DIAGONAL TO FIND THE HIDDEN WORDS.

```
A  S  M  E  D  I  T  A  T  E  C
X  T  Y  E  N  B  P  A  U  E  E
Z  A  R  L  O  P  E  D  G  N  A
Y  R  L  O  R  L  S  T  I  O  Q
N  A  R  E  N  A  U  R  G  U  Q
O  N  S  U  R  J  C  A  R  G  U
M  I  N  D  F  U  L  N  E  S  S
R  U  L  U  C  E  Y  Q  S  N  S
A  S  K  I  G  B  V  U  T  N  T
H  R  Z  E  N  J  F  I  L  K  W
C  A  L  M  O  I  Y  L  O  E  D
```

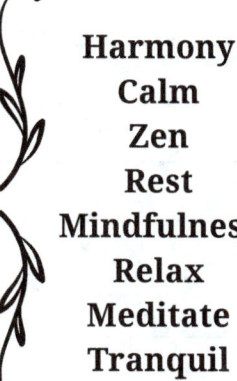

Harmony
Calm
Zen
Rest
Mindfulness
Relax
Meditate
Tranquil

NOTES TO SELF

_____

_____

_____

_____

_____

_____

_____

_____

_____

_____

_____

_____

_____

_____

_____

_____

_____

_____

Day 18

I am worthy
of success.

BELIEVING IN YOURSELF

Have you ever found yourself on the path to reaching your goals, only to be suddenly visited by those sneaky doubts inside your head? Oh, I've definitely been there. One of the biggest ones for me has always been this persistent little voice asking, **"Am I really worthy of success?"**

Self-doubt can be a significant barrier to success. It often leads to procrastination, fear of failure, and even self-sabotage. For example, have you ever faced a setback and felt like it was the end of the world? We've all been there. But here's a game-changing perspective: What if we viewed failures as learning opportunities or stepping stones? A strong self-worth means recognizing that your value does not diminish because of a misstep or a temporary defeat. It's knowing deep down that you're deserving of success, no matter the hurdles.

Remember, each setback is a setup for a comeback. It's an opportunity to learn, grow, and emerge stronger. So, the next time you face a challenge and doubt creeps in, remind yourself: "I've got this!" **You are worthy of success**, and it's time to start believing it.

List three goals you are currently aiming to achieve.

♥

· ·

♥

· ·

♥

· ·

Write a note about why you're worthy of achieving these goals.

Write today's affirmation five times.

"I am worthy of success."

NOTES TO SELF

Day 19

Settling is <u>not</u> an option.

LIVE A LIFE YOU LOVE

Have you ever caught yourself accepting less than you deserve? Settling can often feel like the easy or safe option, but it usually stems from a fear of the unknown, what others will think, or even a lapse in recognizing our self-worth. It may be staying in a job that doesn't fulfill you, remaining in a toxic relationship, or shrinking your dreams to fit into someone else's idea of what's possible. Consider why you might be settling in certain areas of your life. Is it fear of the unknown, comfort in familiarity, or a belief that you don't deserve better?

Well, here's the truth: **you are worthy of more, so much more. You deserve a life filled with love, success, happiness, and respect**, so don't settle for a life that's merely okay when it has the potential to be extraordinary.

It takes courage to step out of your comfort zone, but when you dare to leap toward your true potential, you unlock a world of possibilities that fills you with joy.

So, never settle for less than you deserve because the right opportunities and people will recognize and celebrate that worth.

Consider why you might be settling in some areas of your life. What steps can you take to move closer to what you truly deserve?

Write today's affirmation five times.

"Settling is not an option."

NOTES TO SELF

_____

_____

_____

_____

_____

_____

_____

_____

_____

_____

_____

_____

_____

_____

_____

_____

_____

_____

Day 20

I welcome good things into my life.

MANIFESTING MAGIC

Have you ever felt like you're just one step away from unlocking an abundance of good things in your life? That's the **magic of manifesting** – the art of bringing your deepest desires and dreams into reality.

The foundation of manifesting lies in the power of your thoughts; when you consistently focus on positive outcomes and visualize your goals and dreams as vividly and in as much detail as possible, you set the stage for them to unfold.

Be clear about what you want to achieve. Instead of, "I want to be happy," be specific – what exactly does happiness mean to you? Is it a fulfilling job, a loving relationship, better health? Specific intentions set a clear direction for your energy to flow. Acknowledge your worth, too. Then, be open to opportunities. **Sometimes, the universe has even better plans than we do.**

By embracing these principles, you can let the good things you've been dreaming of flow effortlessly into your life. Remember, the universe is abundant, and it's waiting to shower you with its gifts – all you need to do is ask and be ready to receive.

What are your biggest desires and dreams? What would your ideal life look like in five years? It is time to manifest it.

NOTES TO SELF

_____

_____

_____

_____

_____

_____

_____

_____

_____

_____

_____

_____

_____

_____

_____

_____

Day 21

I do things that nourish my soul.

WHAT LIGHTS YOU UP?

You know how it goes – we're always on this non-stop treadmill between school, work, and personal stuff. And in all that hustle, it's easy to forget about doing the activities that bring joy and peace to our souls.

Taking care of ourselves keeps us connected to who we really are. And honestly, **when our soul is happy, everything else seems to fall into place, doesn't it?** What brings you joy might be those quiet moments in the morning with a cup of coffee, or maybe it's getting lost in a good book, gardening, or dancing alone in your bedroom to your favorite songs.

I've realized how important it is to make time for these things. It's like giving our inner selves a big, warm hug. When we don't, we can feel a bit off. Like something's missing, even when everything else in life seems okay. Nourishing our souls is what keeps us grounded. Here's a little nudge: It's time to **do more of what lights you up.**

What self-care activities bring you happiness? List them below, and promise to do more of these things.

Write today's affirmation five times.

"I do things that nourish my soul."

NOTES TO SELF

Day 22

I release the need to be perfect.

PROGRESS NOT PERFECTION

For the longest time, I strived for perfection in my work, relationships, appearance, and even my thoughts. It was exhausting! The constant pressure to meet an impossible standard left me feeling inadequate and overwhelmed. I realized perfectionism is a moving goal post where satisfaction is just out of reach.

But my world shifted when I started embracing my humanity, and that we all make mistakes, and that's perfectly okay. I'm still a work in progress, and part of that journey includes learning to release my hold on perfectionism. Here are some strategies I've been embracing lately:

- **Self-Compassion:** Recognize that being hard on yourself for not achieving perfection only leads to more stress. Be kind to yourself
- **View Life as Wins and Lessons:** Use mistakes as learning opportunities and remember to celebrate progress - NOT perfection.
- **Seek Support:** Talk about your struggle with perfectionism; sometimes, just voicing these feelings can be incredibly liberating.

List the achievements you're proud of, both big and small. Then, take a moment to celebrate the hard work you've put in and the progress you've made.

Write today's affirmation five times.

"I release the need to be perfect."

NOTES TO SELF

_____

_____

_____

_____

_____

_____

_____

_____

_____

_____

_____

_____

_____

_____

_____

_____

Day 23

I am valuable and deserving of love.

FINDING THE LOVE YOU DESERVE

When it comes to love and relationships, many of us, at some point, have faced the dilemma of choosing between being alone or settling for a relationship that doesn't quite fulfill us. Breakups suck, I know. But it is far better to be alone and at peace with oneself than to feel lonely and unfulfilled in a relationship that doesn't meet your emotional needs.

Love, the deep, meaningful, and genuine kind, is worth waiting for. It's about finding someone who cherishes you for who you are and aligns with your values and dreams. The right love will enhance your life, not complete it. You're whole all by yourself. It might feel disheartening sometimes, especially when you haven't found that special someone yet, but trust me, your time will come.

When you truly understand your worth, the idea of settling for a relationship that offers anything less becomes unacceptable. So, if love hasn't found you yet, don't lose hope or think any less of yourself. You are a valuable and remarkable person deserving of love.

Write a love letter to yourself, highlighting what you genuinely deserve in love and relationships, and establish what you will no longer accept.

NOTES TO SELF

_____

_____

_____

_____

_____

_____

_____

_____

_____

_____

_____

_____

_____

_____

_____

_____

_____

_____

Day 24

My needs are important.

TAKING CARE OF YOU

It can be so easy to put ourselves last on the to-do list. But here's a little reminder (*yes, I'm going to repeat it*): **taking care of your needs isn't selfish; it's essential.** And guess what? You don't need to feel guilty about it because your needs are just as valid as anyone else's.

Prioritizing self-care not only makes us happier and more productive, but it also benefits those around us.

I learned this firsthand when I started setting aside time each week for a quiet walk in the park. Simply spending time in nature - even for just ten minutes - helps me recharge.

Acknowledging that your needs are important needs, whether that means taking some alone time, a break from work, or seeking emotional support, is a powerful way to show yourself respect. Self-care may even involve declining requests or opportunities that sap your energy. If you often struggle with saying 'no,' start practicing assertiveness in small, manageable steps. Remind yourself of what's important to you and the worth of your time. Those who care for you will honor your boundaries, and by prioritizing your own well-being, you gain the energy and capacity to care for others, if and when you choose to do so.

Identify the areas where you find it challenging to establish boundaries or tend to neglect your own needs. Reflect on the reasons behind these struggles.

Write today's affirmation five times.

"My needs are important."

NOTES TO SELF

Day 25

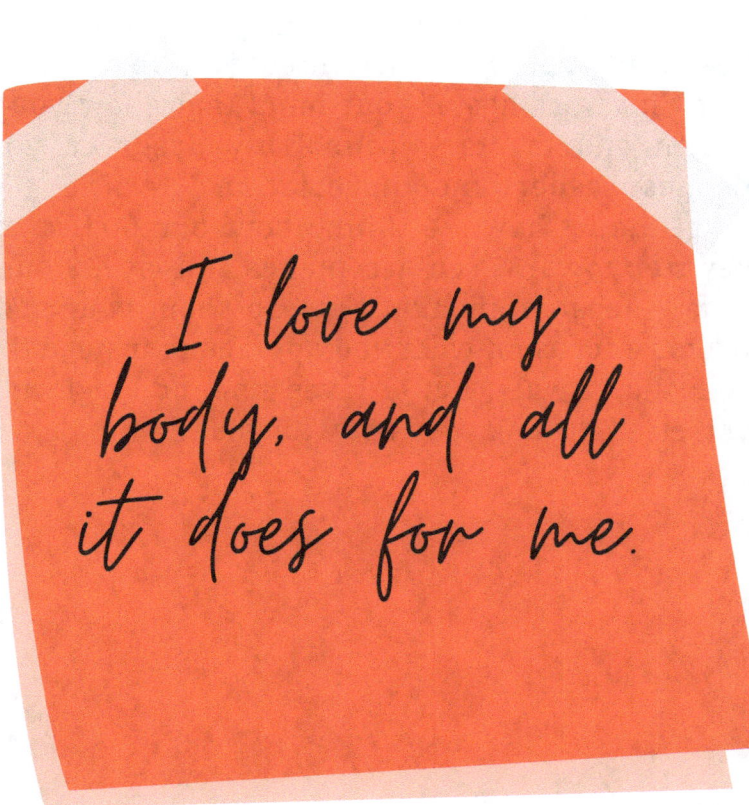

I love my body, and all it does for me.

CELEBRATING YOUR BODY

Social media often highlights picture-perfect lifestyles and bodies, so it's easy to focus on perceived flaws or compare ourselves to others. However, we need to start viewing our bodies as the amazing entities they are, worthy of our love and care.

Each body is unique, with its own shape, size, and story; it allows you to experience the world, interact with loved ones, and pursue your passions. From the strength in your muscles that lets you engage in activities you love to the intricate workings of your mind that allow you to dream and create – **your body deserves your deepest respect and appreciation.**

Reframing how we think about our bodies is a key step towards self-acceptance and love. So next time a negative thought pops up about your body, try to re-focus on what you appreciate instead. Did you take a walk, hug a loved one, or laugh until you cried? Thank your body for that.

Think about a favorite memory. How did your body help you experience or achieve this moment?

> **Write today's affirmation five times.**
> **"I love my body, and all it does for me."**

NOTES TO SELF

Day 26

I boldly and unapologetically take up space.

STAND TALL, SPEAK LOUD

Taking up space is about more than physical presence; it's about making your presence known, your opinions heard, and your contributions felt. It's about stepping into a room and owning your right to be there - whether in a meeting, a social setting, or even in expressing your creativity. How often have you held back from saying or writing something, fearing it might not be meaningful enough or well-received? Well, let me tell you that while writing my memoir, *I Blew Up My Life, and I've Never Been Happier*, there were moments filled with doubt and hesitation. I wondered if people would even care. However, once the memoir was published, people from all over the world reached out to share how my story resonated with them and gave them the courage to face their own fears. I sometimes wonder, what if I had let my fears hold me back? What if I hadn't shared my story with the world? Guess we'll never know.

All that to say, your perspectives and ideas are valuable. And even when it's uncomfortable or intimidating, **using your voice for good is a powerful way to make an impact.** After all, the world needs what only you can offer. You got this!

Recall a moment when you boldly took up space, where you felt confident and unapologetic in expressing yourself. Describe how it felt.

BE BOLD: WORD SEARCH

INSTRUCTIONS: SEARCH UP, DOWN, FORWARD, BACKWARD, AND DIAGONAL TO FIND THE HIDDEN WORDS.

```
E M P O W E R J E V T
X C Y E N B P A U O P
H A O L O O E D G I I
T R L U R A S Y I C H
G A R E R A C R G E B
N N S U R A C A V G O
E X N D C U G A B S L
R U L O C E R E S N D
T S V I G B V U T N A
S D Z E I M P A C T G
A C O N F I D E N C E
```

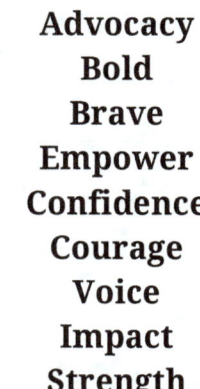

Advocacy
Bold
Brave
Empower
Confidence
Courage
Voice
Impact
Strength

NOTES TO SELF

_____

_____

_____

_____

_____

_____

_____

_____

_____

_____

_____

_____

_____

_____

_____

_____

_____

_____

_____

Day 27

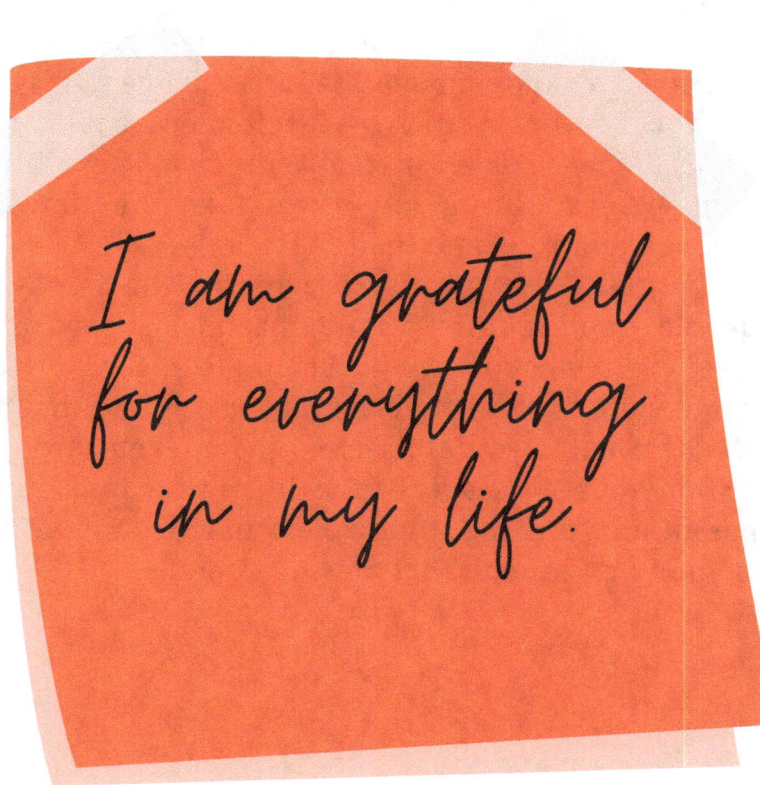

I am grateful for everything in my life.

ATTITUDE OF GRATITUDE

Turns out, appreciating the little things in life can make a big difference in our overall happiness.

Gratitude is like a magic lens that changes how we see things. It's about noticing and appreciating the small stuff – like having a good WiFi connection when you're streaming your favorite show or that cozy feeling of sipping a hot chocolate on a cold day. **Science says that focusing on the good stuff makes us feel happier and less stressed.** Pretty cool, right?

Life is full of wonders that we sometimes overlook: a random compliment someone gave you on your outfit, your dog's excitement when you come home, or even a good hair day. These little moments can bring joy if we take the time to notice and appreciate them.

Gratitude also means recognizing the fantastic people in your life: family, friends, co-workers, teachers – anyone who's been there for you or made your day a little brighter. Taking the time to let them know you appreciate them, even through a simple text message, can be incredibly impactful, potentially turning their whole day around. (This is your sign to send that message now.)

Look around you.
List ten things you're grateful for.

Write today's affirmation five times.

"I am grateful for everything in my life."

NOTES TO SELF

_____

_____

_____

_____

_____

_____

_____

_____

_____

_____

_____

_____

_____

_____

_____

_____

_____

_____

Day 28

I radiate love.

THE RIPPLE EFFECT

Radiating love starts from within, but imagine the ripple effect when each of us chooses to act, speak, and think with love. Spreading love, even through simple acts of kindness, can brighten someone's day and inspire others to do the same, creating a cycle of positivity.

I encourage you to consciously **choose love** in your interactions daily, whether with a warm smile or a heartfelt 'thank you.' You can create a wave of positivity that can **change the world**. After all, every bit of love counts in a world that can always use more kindness.

Just as important as spreading love to others is showing that same love to ourselves. Often, we are our own harshest critics, forgetting that we deserve kindness and compassion. Showing yourself love can be as simple as acknowledging your achievements, allowing yourself time to rest, or engaging in activities that bring you joy. In essence, by embracing and sharing love in its many forms, both with others and ourselves, we create a world brimming with compassion and understanding.

Reflect on a time when you felt truly loved or extended love to someone else. How did it make you feel?

Write today's affirmation five times.

"I radiate love."

NOTES TO SELF

_____

_____

_____

_____

_____

_____

_____

_____

_____

_____

_____

_____

_____

_____

_____

_____

_____

Day 29

I am blessed with supportive friends.

I'LL BE THERE FOR YOU

There's something truly magical about having friends who genuinely support you. These are the people who celebrate your successes without a hint of envy and are there to lift you up when you're down. They're the ones who listen to your dreams, no matter how big or wild, and say, "Go for it!" instead of, "Be realistic." They're the cheerleaders who make life more fun and full of endless joy. These are not so-called "yes" people; they challenge you, help you grow, and remind you of your worth even when you forget.

On the flip side, there's the tougher aspect of friendships – recognizing when someone is dragging you down. It's a tough pill to swallow, but not everyone deserves a front-row seat in your life. **It's okay to outgrow people** who don't support your growth. Letting go doesn't mean you're a terrible person; it means protecting your peace and investing your energy in reciprocal and uplifting relationships.

Take time to cherish those who cherish us and let go of those who don't contribute to our growth. It is okay to be selective about who you let into your life. **After all, you deserve friends as extraordinary as you are.**

Name three people in your life that lift you up. Find a way to show them appreciation this week.

♥
. . . .
♥
. . . .
♥
. . . .

Now, reach out to two or three friends. Ask them to describe you in three words or adjectives. Write the words below.

NOTES TO SELF

_____
_____
_____
_____
_____
_____
_____
_____
_____
_____
_____
_____
_____
_____
_____
_____
_____
_____

Day 30

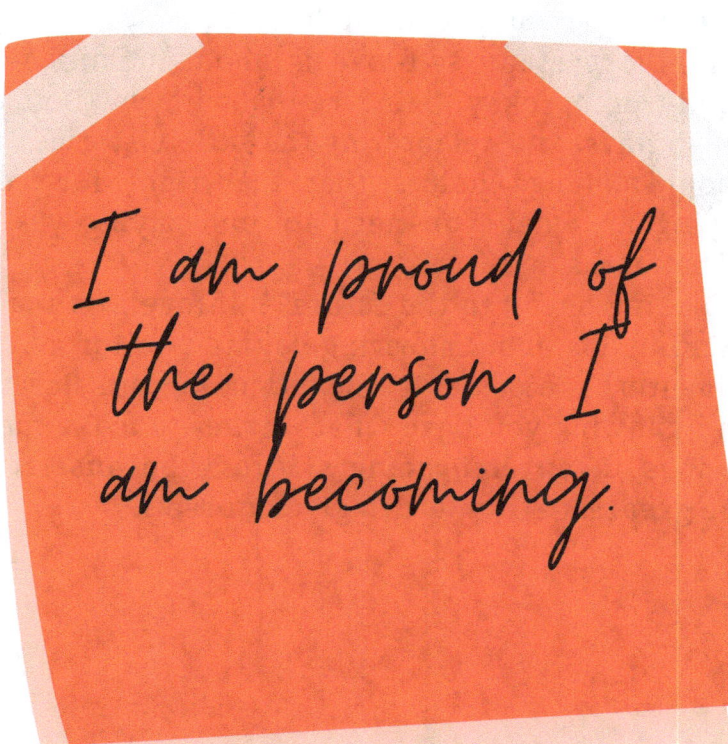

I am proud of the person I am becoming.

HEAL. LOVE. GROW.

Self-love is about being kind to ourselves through every chapter of our story — embracing where we've been, loving where we are, and getting excited about where we're going.

When it comes to the past, give yourself a big, understanding hug for everything you've been through, acknowledging that, "Yep, I made some mistakes, but hey, I learned a lot." It's about not being too hard on yourself for the bumps along the way because they actually shaped you into the awesome person you are today.

In the present, self-love is about making sure you're doing okay, being gentle with yourself on tough days, and celebrating the little victories. It's about making choices that feel right for you, saying no when you need to, and saying yes to what sparks joy.

Looking ahead to the future, self-love gets really exciting. It's about cheering yourself on for all the adventures to come. It's believing in your dreams and knowing you have what it takes to make them happen. **Keep embracing self-love because it is the greatest gift you can give yourself.**

Finish the prompt: At this moment, I would like to tell my younger self...

To my future self, I would like to say...

To my present self, I am proud of you because...

NOTES TO SELF

_____

_____

_____

_____

_____

_____

_____

_____

_____

_____

_____

_____

_____

_____

_____

_____

_____

_____

HELLO, AGAIN.

A FINAL NOTE

Congratulations on completing *Love Notes To Self*! This past month, you've embarked on a profoundly personal exploration of self-love.

Reflecting on this journey, how has your mindset evolved? I hope you've noticed firsthand how self-love and appreciation can change your life.

Now, you might be wondering, **"What's next?"** Well, the beauty of this journey is its infinite nature. You can start over, revisiting each prompt with fresh eyes and a new perspective. Your responses might change, reflecting your own personal growth. Remember, self-love is a practice, and, like any practice, it becomes richer with time; every day presents another opportunity to be kind to yourself, recognize your worth, and grow in ways you never thought possible.

If this journal **sparked joy** in your life, consider giving a copy to a friend who could benefit from its empowering journey.

Now, I'll leave you with one final reminder: **Celebrate yourself every day because you, more than anyone else, deserve your love and affection.**

Amber James
xoxo

Author, Creator of Notes To Self Shop

LOVE NOTES TO SELF

Time to write your own **"notes to self."** And don't forget to tag **@NotesToSelfShop** on Instagram with your messages for the chance to be featured on our page.

Thank you for supporting my dreams! By purchasing **Notes To Self Shop** products, you have helped a woman-owned business.

Learn more at:
www.NotesToSelfShop.com

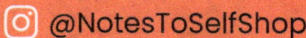 @NotesToSelfShop

ABOUT THE AUTHOR

Amber James is the creator of Notes To Self Shop and author of *I Blew Up My Life, And I've Never Been Happier* and *Notes to Self: 30-Day Guided Journal*. Her work has appeared on CNN, MTV, Huffington Post, and AOL. She holds a degree in journalism from Ohio University and currently lives in Pittsburgh with her pup, Penny Lane.

Connect With Amber
Instagram and TikTok: @NotesToSelfShop
http://www.NotesToSelfShop.com